BOOK OF MORMON STORIES APPLIED TO CHILDREN

WHO'S YOUR HERO?

THE ULTIMATE COLLECTION
VOLUME 1

written and illustrated by
DAVID BOWMAN

Dedicated to my five little "heroes"
Baylee, Kambria, Lydia, Caleb, and Colton

ISBN: 978-1-60907-864-5

SKU: 5119163

Printed in China

RR Donnelley, Shenzhen, China   01/19

10   9   8   7   6   5   4   3

"For I did liken all scriptures unto us,
that it might be for our profit and learning."
—Nephi

Author's Note to Kids:

The prophet has asked all the youth in the church to learn and love some specific scriptures. They are called Scripture Mastery verses. You are not too young to start learning and loving them too! So, each hero in this book has one scripture mastery to go with his/her story. We'll call them SCRIPTURE POWER verses!! See how many of these SCRIPTURE POWER verses YOU can learn (especially the highlighted part)! Go for it!

Author's Note to Parents:

Who's Your Hero? is both an enjoyable children's book and a teaching tool. The "How can YOU be like . . . " pages and Family Home Evening Lesson Helps are designed to help you teach your children how the principles found within each story apply to them. I encourage you to take full advantage of these tools and watch how the heroes from the Book of Mormon come to life for your young ones. God bless.

David Bowman

NEPHI
Never Complains

Scripture Power!

And it came to pass that I, Nephi, said unto my father: I will go and do the things which the Lord hath commanded, for I know that the Lord giveth no commandments unto the children of men, save he shall prepare a way for them that they may accomplish the thing which he commandeth them.

—1 Nephi 3:7

Hello, friend! My name is Nephi.

I want to tell you about the journey I made with my family to the Promised Land. It was during our travels that I learned that I am happier when I DON'T COMPLAIN.

One night, my father, Lehi, was praying. He was sad because the people in our city were very wicked. The Lord told Lehi to leave the city and take our family into the wilderness.

(1 Nephi 1:5; 2:2–3)

Father told the whole family what the Lord had commanded us to do. "Okay," I said. I wanted to obey my parents and the Lord. Two of my older brothers, Laman and Lemuel, complained! "But we don't want to leave our house and all of our things," they argued. (1 Nephi 2:11–12; 3:16)

3

Our family and some of our friends left our homes and went into the wilderness. Many days later, my brothers and I were hunting. That was the only way to get food for our family. Suddenly, my bow broke! (1 Nephi 16:17–18)

Laman and Lemuel were very angry with me. We had no food, and everyone was hungry. Many of the family members began to complain. (1 Nephi 16:18–20)

Instead of complaining, I chose to follow the Spirit and make a new bow. (1 Nephi 16:23)

With my new bow, I was able to get food for everyone. We were all very happy and gave thanks to the Lord. (1 Nephi 16:31–32)

After many years traveling in the wilderness, we came to the ocean. Early one morning, I was praying on top of a high mountain. The Lord commanded me to build a ship so that we could sail to the Promised Land. (1 Nephi 17:4–5, 7–8)

Even though I had never built a ship, I didn't complain. I was happy to obey because I knew the Lord would help me. (1 Nephi 17:9–10, 15)

But Laman and Lemuel did not want to help me. "That sounds too hard!" they murmured.

(1 Nephi 17:17–18)

I encouraged my brothers to help and told them it was a commandment from the Lord.
They decided to be helpers and have a good attitude. At last, the ship was finished. Hooray!

(1 Nephi 17:49; 18:1, 4)

We sailed across the ocean until we arrived in the Promised Land. I learned that when we obey without complaining, Heavenly Father blesses us and everyone is happier. (1 Nephi 18:8, 23)

How can YOU be like Nephi and never complain?

THEN

NOW

"I will go and do the things which the Lord hath commanded"

When your parents ask you to do something you might not want to do, instead of arguing, obey with a good attitude!

When something goes wrong in your family, look for ways to help instead of reasons to complain.

Put on a happy face and say, "Okay!" when you are asked to do something that is hard—even if others are complaining.

Your happy attitude will help them want to obey, too!

Songs and Hymns

Children's Songbook:
"Book of Mormon Stories," pp. 118–19
(additional verse by David Bowman)
The Lord commanded Lehi to leave Jerusalem.
Laman and Lemuel complained and said, "This is no fun!"
Nephi trusted in the Lord and obeyed happily.
He taught us how to live righteously.
"Nephi's Courage," p. 120
"Quickly I'll Obey," p. 197
"When We're Helping," p. 198

LDS Hymns:
"There Is Sunshine in My Soul Today," no. 227
"Put Your Shoulder to the Wheel," no. 252
"Love at Home," no. 294

Scriptures on Being Obedient with a Positive Attitude

D&C 58:26–27, 29
D&C 64:33–34
2 Corinthians 9:7
Psalm 100:2
1 Nephi 3:6

Note: You can put the scriptural references on sticky notes and attach them in the pages of this book where it describes Nephi not complaining. The children can find the sticky notes, look up the scripture (individually or as a family), and then discuss how the example applies to them.

Other Scripture Stories on This Topic

Positive Example: Abraham commanded to sacrifice Isaac (Genesis 22)

Negative Example: Children of Israel murmuring in the wilderness (Exodus 15:22–27; 16:1–15; 17:1–7)

Quotes from the Prophets and Apostles

"Remember, a good attitude produces good results, a fair attitude fair results, a poor attitude poor results. We each shape our own life, and the shape of it is determined largely by our attitude."
Elder M. Russell Ballard
"Providing for Our Needs," *Ensign,* May 1981, p. 86.

"Instead of murmuring . . . being of good cheer is what is needed, and being of good cheer is . . . contagious."
Elder Neal A. Maxwell
"'Murmur Not,'" *Ensign,* November 1989, p. 84.

Stories and Messages from *The Friend* Magazine

"Ben's Busy Day" (*The Friend,* January 2005, p. 40)

"Dishing up Blessings" (*The Friend,* November 2004, p. 29)

Activities

Write a Letter
Have each child write a letter to Nephi, telling him how he or she has followed (or will follow) Nephi's example by not complaining. The next family home evening, deliver letters to the children that "Nephi" (aka—Mom or Dad) has written back to each child, commending them for their behavior.

You Draw the Story
Read the "How you can be like Nephi" pages together. Then, have each child draw his or her *own* page of specific ways he or she can follow (or has recently followed) Nephi's example by not complaining. Tuck the drawings into the book or put them on the refrigerator as reminders to try to be like Nephi.

Thumbs Up!
Photocopy and cut out several of the "thumbs up" taken from the story (see page 166). Each child comes up with 1–3 scenarios in which they could obey Mom or Dad (or Heavenly Father) without complaining, arguing, or whining. Role-play their scenarios and then give them a "thumbs up" for each positive response. Then, throughout the next week (or longer) give a "thumbs up" to the children (and Dad) each time you feel they have obeyed *WITH a positive attitude.* Offer some sort of reward for a certain number of "thumbs up" earned.

Act It Out
"Nephi and the Broken Bow" (1 Nephi 16:15–32) is a great story to act out with the family! Gather as many props as you can muster up (bathrobes, towels for head-dresses, a bow and arrow, a ball for the Liahona, stuffed animals to hunt, etc.). Assign family members different roles and choose a narrator. He or she can read the story from the scriptures (or, with younger families, Mom or Dad could simply use this book or tell the story in their own words) while the family acts it out. Afterward, discuss the lessons we can learn from the story (i.e. Murmuring doesn't help anything and is contagious . . . You can CHOOSE not to complain . . . Nephi's respect for his father).

Build a Ship
Construct your own boats-bound-for-the-Promised-Land out of Popsicle sticks and glue (or any other materials). Discuss how each piece of wood is like each good deed we do in building the "ships of our character."

LEHI'S FAMILY

(Most of Them)

Holds Fast to the Word of God

Scripture Power!

Thy word is a lamp unto my feet, and a light unto my path.
—Psalms 119:105

Greetings, friend! It's me, Lehi. One night, while my family and I were traveling through the wilderness, I had a special dream. It showed me how important it is to always HOLD FAST to the WORD of GOD.

In my dream I saw a huge field with many, many people. They were all trying to get to a tree that had white fruit. However, the fruit was not easy to get to! There were many ways for the people to get lost or distracted. (1 Nephi 8:2, 9–10)

I saw that the only ones who made it to the tree HELD FAST to a ROD of IRON the entire way.

(1 Nephi 8:30)

I walked up to the tree, pulled off a piece of fruit, and took a bite. It was delicious! It made me feel very good inside. More than anything, I wanted to share this fruit with my family. I looked around for them and saw my wife and sons far away. I waved for them to come and join me. (1 Nephi 8:11–15)

My wife, Sariah, and my two sons, Nephi and Sam, saw me waving and said, "Yes, we're coming!" But Laman and Lemuel, my two oldest sons, did not want to come. (Sigh!) Even in my dream they were acting like knuckleheads. (1 Nephi 8:16–18)

Nephi, Sariah, and Sam began their journey to the tree. The first thing they did was GRAB HOLD of the IRON ROD. It led them along a narrow path that would take them to the tree. With each step, they held on as tight as they could to the iron rod. (1 Nephi 8:14–16, 19–22)

26

Suddenly a thick mist of darkness surrounded my family! They couldn't see where they were going! So they gripped the iron rod even *tighter,* trusting that it would lead them to the tree. Other people who would not HOLD to the ROD wandered off and were lost in the darkness. (1 Nephi 8:23)

Next I saw a huge building filled with people in expensive clothes. They were laughing and trying to get those on the path to join them. To some, it looked like those people were having much more fun! They let go of the iron rod and started going toward the building. But instead they fell into a river of filthy water and drowned. (1 Nephi 8:26–27, 31–32)

My family followed the iron rod until they could finally see the tree. They had made it! Hooray! They saw people happily picking and eating the fruit. (1 Nephi 8:24)

Unfortunately, some of those people looked over toward the huge building. They saw the people in the building laughing and making fun of them for eating the fruit. Embarrassed, they tossed their fruit aside, walked away from the tree, and were lost. Can you believe it? (1 Nephi 8:25–28)

Nephi, Sam, Sariah, and I were not embarrassed. We enjoyed eating the fruit together and paid no attention to the people in the building. I was so happy to have my family there with me, even though I was very sad that Laman and Lemuel would not come. And I was grateful for the iron rod—without HOLDING FAST to the IRON ROD, we never could have made it to the tree. (1 Nephi 8:16, 35)

31

And then I woke up. I knew that this dream was from Heavenly Father and that it had special meaning. The things I saw in my dream were **symbols**. Here is what those symbols mean and how this dream can help you.

The tree is **God's love** (1 Nephi 11:21–23).

To eat the fruit is to **feel Heavenly Father's love** for you. It's the best feeling in the world!

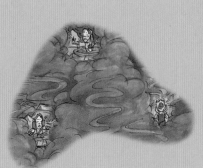

The mists of darkness are **temptations** (1 Nephi 12:17),

the huge building is **pride** and **worldliness** (1 Nephi 11:36),

and the filthy river is **sin** (1 Nephi 12:16),

. . . all of which keep us from feeling **God's love** (eating the fruit).

There's only one way to make it past all those bad influences—HOLD FAST to the IRON ROD!

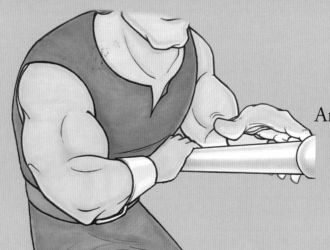

And the IRON ROD is the **word of God** (1 Nephi 15:23–24).

The **word of God** comes from the **scriptures,** the **words of the prophets and apostles**, and **the Holy Ghost**.

We HOLD FAST to the **word of God** when we *do* what the scriptures and the prophets tell us to do and when we obey the promptings of the Holy Ghost.

How can YOU be like Lehi and his family and hold fast to the word of God?

"Thy word is a lamp unto my feet, and a light unto my path."

33

When you HOLD to the ROD, you won't be tempted to make bad choices.

When you HOLD to the ROD, you won't feel like you *have* to *have* all the latest and greatest toys.

35

When you HOLD to the ROD, you won't be ashamed or embarrassed if people make fun of you for your beliefs.

When you HOLD to the ROD and stay away from Satan's influences, you will feel Heavenly Father's love for you. You will be happy and know you are doing the right thing.

FHE Lesson Helps for Lehi's Family Holds Fast to the Word of God

Songs and Hymns

Children's Songbook:
    "Book of Mormon Stories," 118–19 (additional verse by David Bowman)

> *Lehi had a dream one night that's meant for you and me:*
> *Holding to an iron rod he made it to a tree.*
> *Its fruit he ate, it tasted great, he knew the iron rod*
> *For you and me had to be the Word of God.*

    "Search, Ponder, and Pray," 109
    "Follow the Prophet," 110–11

The Friend:
    "Scripture Power," Clive Romney, October 1987, 10–11

LDS Hymns:
    "The Iron Rod," no. 274
    "As I Search the Holy Scriptures," no. 277
    "Thy Holy Word," no. 279

Scriptures on Holding Fast to the Word of God

Joshua 1:8
2 Timothy 3:16
1 Nephi 15:23–24
Alma 31:5
Helaman 3:29

Other Scripture Stories on This Topic

Alma and the sons of Mosiah search the scriptures diligently on their missions (Alma 17:1–4)

Quotes from General Authorities

"I hope that for you [scripture study] . . . will become something far more enjoyable than a duty. . . . I promise you that as you read, your minds will be enlightened and your spirits will be lifted."
    President Gordon B. Hinckley
    "The Light within You," *Ensign,* May 1995, 99

"I plead with you to make time for immersing yourselves in the scriptures. Couple scripture study with your prayers."
    Elder M. Russell Ballard
    "Be Strong in the Lord and in the Power of His Might," CES Fireside for Young Adults, 3 March 2002

Stories and Messages from *The Friend* Magazine

"The Right Path," Ray Goldrup, May 2006, 36–39

"Hold On," Elizabeth Giles, September 2006, 11

Activities

Lehi Says . . .

This is a good old-fashioned game of Simon (in this case, Lehi) Says. To play this game, every family member needs to have a Book of Mormon or set of scriptures. Dad will act as "Lehi." The first thing he says is "Lehi says . . . Pick up your scriptures and don't let go." Then he makes several "Lehi says" statements (whatever Dad comes up with). After a while he tries to trick them with "set your book down at your feet" or "put your scriptures on the couch," without saying "Lehi says." Play as long as you'd like, periodically trying to get them to let go of their books.

Discussion: Lehi is a prophet, and prophets always encourage us to Hold to the Iron Rod (the scriptures) and never let go. In other words, if someone or something tries to get you to disobey the commandments (to let go of the iron rod or the word of God), then you can know that that influence is coming from Satan and you should not listen. If you will follow what "Lehi (the prophet) says," you will be safe. Use pages 12–13 of this book to help with the discussion.

Find the Fruit

Beforehand, hide one piece of fruit for each family member in or by various locations in the house listed below (pick locations that apply to your house). During the activity, give each family member a secret code of numbers indicating where their fruit is hidden. Tell them they will use the word of God in 1 Nephi 8 (Lehi's vision) to decipher the code and discover the clue words needed to find their fruit. Then teach them the key to breaking the code: 1st number = the verse in chapter 8, 2nd number = the line in that verse, 3rd number = the word in that line.

    13–4–1, 20–5–4 (kitchen sink)
    24–2–2, 19–1–7 (clothing iron)
    14–4–6, 27–3–6 (Mom's dresses/closet)
    2–2–2, 5–3–2 (Dad's bathrobe pocket)
    19–1–5, 8–5–2, 13–1–4 (fishing pole)
    2–2–2, 30–1–6 (Dad's desk)
    30–1–4, 21–2–3, 26–4–2 (doll house/action figure castle)
    2–2–2, 14–4–1, 2–4–2 (Dad's pillow)

Once everyone has found his or her fruit, eat it together in the family room. Discuss how delicious it is, how it is "like feeling God's love for us and how much we want to work together as a family to feel God's love in our home." Also discuss how it was only by following God's word (the secret code) that you were able to find His love (the fruit).

Word Search

On page 167 of this book is a WORD SEARCH of different sources where we can find the word of God. Children can work together to solve the puzzle in the book or you can make copies for them to do individually. Discuss with them how each of these sources (books, people, etc.) can reveal God's word to us today.

ENOS
Prays Sincerely

Scripture Power!

If any of you lack wisdom, let him ask of God, that giveth to all men liberally, and upbraideth not; and it shall be given him.

But let him ask in faith, nothing wavering. For he that wavereth is like a wave of the sea driven with the wind and tossed.
—James 1:5-6

Hey, friend! My name is Enos.

I want to tell you about the time I learned to PRAY SINCERELY.

One day, I hiked into the forest to go hunting. "See you later, Mom and Dad!" I waved. "Goodbye, son . . . be careful," my parents replied. (Enos 1:3)

While I was exploring, I started thinking of my dad and how he always taught me about Heavenly Father and Jesus. I felt thankful to have such a great father. (Enos 1:1)

But I wasn't happy like other members of the Church were. My father taught me that the joy they feel comes from obeying the commandments. *I want to feel like that!* I thought. (Enos 1:3)

So I knelt down . . . (Enos 1:4)

. . . and began to pray. I talked to my Heavenly Father all day long . . . (Enos 1:4)

. . . and into the night. I told Him everything I was feeling. I didn't care how long it took. I wanted to feel He was there and to be forgiven of my mistakes. (Enos 1:4)

Suddenly, a very peaceful feeling came over me. I felt a voice inside me say, *Enos, your sins are forgiven because of your faith in Jesus Christ.* I knew Jesus and Heavenly Father were thinking about me and loved me very much. (Enos 1:5–8)

I wanted all my Nephite friends and family to be blessed, so I prayed for them. (Enos 1:9–10)

I even prayed for our enemies, the Lamanites. They were wicked people and were mean to the Nephites. But I knew that they were still children of God, and that God loved them. I prayed that one day they would learn about Jesus and find happiness living His gospel.

50 (Enos 1:11–14, 20)

Heavenly Father promised me that our writings would be kept safe for hundreds of years, until they could be translated into the Book of Mormon. Then, the Lamanite descendants would read that book and begin to believe in Jesus Christ. It was an answer to my prayer.

(Enos 1:16–18)

What a special night! I walked home knowing that when we PRAY SINCERELY to Him, Heavenly Father hears and answers our prayers. (Enos 1:15, 19)

How can YOU pray sincerely like Enos?

THEN

NOW

"If any of you lack wisdom, let him ask of God"

By praying anytime you feel like it, no matter where you are.

By PRAYING SINCERELY and taking the time to say what you really feel.

By kneeling down when you pray.

When you do something wrong, pray and ask Heavenly Father to forgive you.

55

Ask Heavenly Father to bless the people who you love and care about. You can even pray for people who have been mean to you.

Heavenly Father hears and answers our prayers. You can ask Him to help you with anything you need. Then, be sure to thank Him when he does help you!

57

FHE Lesson Helps for Enos Prays Sincerely

Songs and Hymns

Children's Songbook:
    "Book of Mormon Stories," p. 118–119
        (additional verse by David Bowman)
        Enos went into the woods and prayed with all his might.
        He kneeled down and talked to God all day and all that night.
        The Lord answered Enos's prayer and he was filled with peace.
        He showed us how to pray sincerely.
    "A Child's Prayer," p. 12
    "I Pray in Faith," p. 14
    "I Love to Pray," p. 25
LDS Hymns:
    "Did You Think to Pray?" no. 140
    "Sweet Hour of Prayer," no. 142
    "Secret Prayer," no. 144

Scriptures on Praying Sincerely

    Matthew 6:6–8
    2 Nephi 32:8–9
    Alma 34:26 (18–27)
    Alma 37:37
    D&C 19:28

Note: You can put the scriptural references on sticky notes and attach them to the pages of this book where it describes Enos's prayer. The children can find the sticky notes, look up the scripture (individually or as a family), and then discuss how the example applies to them.

Other Scripture Stories on This Topic

Joseph Smith's First Vision (Joseph Smith–History 1:3–20)

Disciples of Jesus pray continually (3 Nephi 19)

Quotes from General Authorities

"Christ encourages us to pray often—in secret, in our families, in our churches, and in our hearts, continually asking specifically for the things we need."
    Elder David E. Sorensen
    "Prayer," *The Friend,* **April 1996, inside front cover.**

"We are privileged to pray daily for the small and great concerns in our lives."
    President James E. Faust
    "The Lifeline of Prayer," *Ensign,* May 2002, p. 60

Stories and Messages from *The Friend* Magazine

"Seeking Him in Prayer" (*The Friend,* February 2006, p. 8)

"Answered Prayer" (*The Friend,* July 2005, p. 8)

"Heavenly Father Hears Me" (*The Friend,* September 2005, p. 19)

Activities

WRITE A LETTER

Have each child write a letter to Enos telling him how he or she has followed (or will) follow his example by PRAYING SINCERELY. Next family home evening, deliver letters to the children that "Enos" (aka—Mom or Dad) has written back to each child, commending them for their behavior.

YOU DRAW THE STORY

Read the "How can YOU be like Enos" pages together. Then, have each child draw his or her own page of specific ways he or she can follow (or has recently followed) Enos's example by PRAYING SINCERELY. Tuck the drawings into the book or put them on the refrigerator as reminders to try to be like Enos.

TALK TO FATHER?

Dad takes a cell phone (if you have one) with him into another room. Each child takes turns calling him up (using your home phone or another cell) and talking to him for at least one full minute. If you don't have a cell phone, hide Dad behind a couch and use empty cans attached by a string. Bring Dad back in and discuss all the ways how the phone call is like praying to Heavenly Father (He loves you and wants to hear from you, but you have to call Him, you can share anything with Him, etc.). Using the Enos Application pages in this book, discuss how the children can pray as Enos did and then come up with additional ways they can improve their communication with Heavenly Father.

PRAYER ROCKS

Have each family member go outside and "hunt" (like Enos went hunting) for *their* Prayer Rock. With markers, paint, glitter, and glue, everyone decorates their Prayer Rock to make it unique to them. Place the Prayer Rock on your pillow as a reminder to pray like Enos before you go to bed each night. Then, before you get into bed, put the rock on the floor so you'll see it or step on it in the morning as a reminder to pray again before you start the day.

BECAUSE . . .

This is a great way to help young people give thought and meaning to the things they are saying in their prayers: Simply add the word "because" at the end of each phrase. "I'm thankful for Mom and Dad" becomes "I'm thankful for Mom and Dad *because* . . ." and then they think of reasons why they are thankful for their parents. "Please bless our living prophet" becomes "Please bless our living prophet *because* . . . he teaches us so many important things" or ". . . *because* we love him very much and he shows us the way to be happy." It is a simple, yet effective way of keeping prayers from becoming too routine. You'll be surprised how well it works . . . try it!

KING BENJAMIN
And His People
Commit to Christ

Scripture Power!

For the natural man is an enemy to God, and has been from the fall of Adam, and will be, forever and ever, unless he yields to the enticings of the Holy Spirit, and putteth off the natural man and becometh a saint through the atonement of Christ the Lord, and becometh as a child, submissive, meek, humble, patient, full of love, willing to submit to all things which the Lord seeth fit to inflict upon him, even as a child doth submit to his father.

—Mosiah 3:19

Greetings, my young friend! My name is King Benjamin.

The most important thing you or I can do is COMMIT TO CHRIST. Here's how I taught my people that truth.

I tried to be a righteous king all of my life. I loved the scriptures and taught my children to search them diligently. As I grew very old, I wanted my son, Mosiah, to become the next king. So, I invited everyone in the land to gather at the temple. There I would make Mosiah the new king and would speak to my people one last time. (Mosiah 1:7-10)

My people came from all over to be at this important event. Each family set up a tent that faced the temple. That way they could sit inside and hear the word of God that I would teach them. They were eager to learn. (Mosiah 2:1, 5-6)

When they had all arrived, I couldn't believe how many families there were! I commanded that a large tower be built so that I could stand on top. Now everyone could see me and hear my message. (Mosiah 2:7)

I taught my people about Jesus Christ. I told them that He would come to earth and suffer for our sins, die for us, and be resurrected. This is called the Atonement. "And because Jesus will do this," I said, "we can all 'put off the natural man'." What is the natural man, you say? Good question! (Mosiah 3:5-11, 19)

The natural man is the part of us that sometimes makes wrong choices. We all have it. Whenever we act mean, selfish, angry, or "fight and quarrel one with another," we are following the natural man. "BUT," I explained to my people, "we can 'put off the natural man' and get rid of that yucky feeling anytime we want… when we let the love of Jesus into our hearts." (Mosiah 3:19, 4:14)

"Then we will want to love and serve each other instead!" I said. "We can serve our brothers and sisters, our parents, or anyone who needs help. That is what makes us happy! Even I, whom you call your king, have spent my whole life serving you. Why? Because when you serve other people, you are actually serving God." (Mosiah 2:16-18, 41, 4:15-16)

At the end of my talk, I invited all of the people to commit to be followers of Jesus Christ by making a covenant with Him. It's called "taking His name upon you." It's a promise for the rest of your life. Everyone there at the temple who was old enough made this covenant with Christ. I knew they had made the best decision they could ever make! (Mosiah 5:5-8, 6:2)

How can YOU commit to Christ like King Benjamin and his people?

THEN

NOW

"Put off the natural man and become a saint through the atonement of Christ"

Gather together as a family to enjoy each General Conference. Get excited about hearing the words of our modern-day prophets and apostles. Listen carefully to their talks and try to do the things they say to do.

When those "natural man" feelings creep into your heart, you just say "Natural Man SCRAM!" Put off YOUR "natural man" by doing things that Jesus would do instead. Like . . .

. . . **C**ompliment instead of criticize. Hug instead of hit. If you are frustrated with someone, stop and think before you say something unkind. Always remember, PEOPLE are more important than THINGS. Natural Man SCRAM!!! ☺

Commit to Christ by making YOUR covenant with Him… through baptism! Prepare for it! Be excited for it! And always keep your promise to Jesus after you are baptized. It's the best decision YOU will ever make.

FHE Lesson Helps for King Benjamin and His People Commit to Christ

Songs and Hymns

Children's Songbook:
"Book of Mormon Stories," pp.118-119
(additional verse by David Bowman)
*King Benjamin was a king who served his people well
Standing on a tower high, Christ's story he did tell
Putting off the "natural man" is what we all can do
When we each commit to Christ, through and through*
"I Want To Live the Gospel," p. 148
"I Pledge Myself to Love the Right," p. 161
"I Will Be Valiant," p. 162

LDS Hymns:
"How Firm a Foundation" #85
"I Believe in Christ" #134
"Choose the Right" #239

Scriptures on Committing to Christ

2 Nephi 31:17-21
(See YOUR Strait & Narrow Journey activity)
Omni 1:26
Helaman 5:12
Mosiah 18:5-17

Quotes from General Authorities

"The greatest blessing of general conference comes to us after the conference is over. Remember the pattern recorded frequently in scripture: we gather to hear the words of the Lord, and we return to our homes to live them"
Elder Robert D. Hales
"General Conference: Strengthening Faith and Testimony," *Ensign,* Nov. 2013, 7.

"Following Christ is not a casual or occasional practice but a continuous commitment and way of life that applies at all times and in all places"
Elder Dallin H. Oaks
"Followers of Christ," *Ensign,* May 2013, 97.

Activities

NATURAL... MAN... SCRAM!
This game is basically hot potato. Find an object (like a stuffed animal, a ball, etc.) and label it The Natural Man. Make it undesirable looking somehow. To play the game, everyone sits in a circle and passes the object around the circle as fast as they can. Each time a person gets The Natural Man, he/she has to say "SCRAM!" as he/she "puts it off" to the next person.

While it is being passed around, have music playing in the background, with one of the family members (the "loser" from the previous round) looking away and hitting the "pause" button at a random point (like in musical chairs). When the music stops, whoever is holding the "Natural Man" is out for one round, becoming the "music stopper" for that round, and the game continues. As you get more advanced, instead of passing The Natural Man around in a circle, toss it to anyone you want in the circle.

Then have a discussion about The Natural Man, based on our Scripture POWER verse Mosiah 3:19. How do we put off The Natural Man? Through Christ and through becoming "as a child" . . . like YOUR little treasures ☺!

Focus on the five child-like attributes mentioned: submissive, meek, humble, patient, full of love

Talk about them. Have children come up with examples of each trait. Write them on strips of paper to be put on your fridge, assigning each attribute for one day of the week. (Submissive – Monday, Meek – Tuesday, etc). Find a fun way to focus on each day's trait throughout the next weeks, keeping track of how kids exemplify that trait that day. (The weekend is for working on all five traits ☺)

YOUR Strait and Narrow Journey

2 Nephi 31:17-21 are some of the greatest scriptures we have about what it means to Commit to Christ. Verse 17 says "Repentance and Baptism" is THE GATE, while verses 18-21 describe how once we have entered in through THE GATE, we must "endure to the end" on THE STRAIT & NARROW PATH. Here is a fun way to role-play that concept with your kiddos:

Before FHE, use masking tape to make a continuous "line" that winds throughout the entire house. Intersperse objects your kids can walk across/balance on (such as 2x4's, broom stick handles, ropes, etc.) throughout your tape line. Be creative! Start this line at one of the kid's bedroom doors (label the door frame with the word "BAPTISM") and finish the line in the kitchen. Along the path, put cards or post-it notes that say "Steadfastness in Christ," "Prefect Brightness of Hope," "Love of God," "Love of All Men," "Feasting Upon the Word of Christ" (make sure there is one note for EACH child).

Have all the children start together in the bedroom. As each of them goes through "the Baptism Gate", Mom gives them a big hug and kiss and tells them how proud she is of their choice to be baptized ☺. Now, it's time for them to, as Johnny Cash would say, "walk the line." Tell them to pick up as many notes along the way as they can. (Also, remind them that it's not just themselves they need to worry about staying on the path, but helping their brothers and sisters to do the same.)

Then, each child has to walk along this strait and narrow path, getting post-it notes as they go. If they step off or lose their balance, they have to hurry and get right back on. While they are journeying along the path, Dad gets to play the part of "the adversary." He can entice them with edible treats that are "off the path." He can have a captivating kids show showing on the TV. He can try to physically pull them off the path. He can put obstacles in their path. He can tickle them. Make it fun. Mom can help Dad or she can help the kids (acting as the Holy Ghost instead).

When they finally arrive in the kitchen, congratulate them and then make the analogy. Read 2 Nephi 31:17-21. Discuss the gate and the path, the adversary's role, the notes they gathered (all the phrases being found in verse 20) and what those phrases mean, etc. The LEHI'S FAMILY Holds Fast to the Word of God story in this book would be a great supplement to this lesson.

And then, the reward of eternal life . . . REFRESHMENTS! ☺

And while we're on the subject...
LOOKING FOR A GREAT BAPTISMAL GIFT?
How about a personalized reminder of their decision to enter through
  "the gate" and live on "the strait and narrow"!

- 8x10 frameable keepsake
- Comes w/cream colored matting
- You add child's photograph
- You add child's name & baptismal date
- Child colors in their own hair color

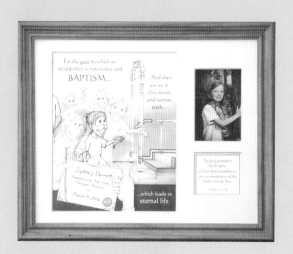

Go to www.whosyourherobooks.com for more details

ABINADI
Shows Courage

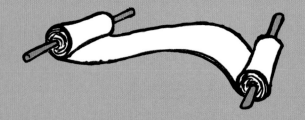

Scripture Power!

I can do all things through Christ which strengtheneth me.
—Philippians 4:13

Greetings, friend! My name is Abinadi.

I want to tell you about my experience with the wicked King Noah. It taught me that we must have COURAGE to stand for what is right.

One day the Lord commanded me to go into the city and tell the people that if they did not repent, they would be destroyed. I did what the Lord commanded me to do, but the people would not listen. Instead, they were angry with me . . . (Mosiah 11:20–21, 26)

. . . and threw me into prison. (Mosiah 12:17)

Then I was taken before King Noah and his priests. They were very wicked men and did not want to repent. Even though it was a scary time, Heavenly Father gave me the COURAGE to answer their questions and condemn their evil ways. (Mosiah 12:17–19)

King Noah didn't believe me. He said, "This man is crazy . . . take him away!" (Mosiah 13:1)

"TOUCH ME NOT!" I exclaimed. As I said this, my face began to shine! I told them that the Lord would protect me until I finished my mission. (Mosiah 13:2–5)

I taught them about Moses and the Ten Commandments. I told them that they needed to repent and keep the commandments. I also taught them about Jesus Christ—-who would come into the world and become our Savior. (Mosiah 13:11–26, 33–35; Mosiah 16:9, 13)

King Noah and his men were very angry at me . . . except for one of the priests. His name was Alma. Alma believed my words and wanted to repent. Alma asked King Noah not to be mad at me . . . (Mosiah 17:1–2)

. . . But, instead, King Noah sent his guards after Alma! Alma ran away as fast as he could.

(Mosiah 17:3–4)

"Abinadi," King Noah sneered at me. "Unless you take back the bad things you said about us, you will be put to death!" (Mosiah 17:7–8)

I would not take back the things I had said because I knew that they were true. I was doing what was right and keeping God's commandment. That was the most important thing . . . even if I had to die for it. (Mosiah 17:9–10, 20)

However, Alma had run away and hidden in the forest. He wrote down the words I had said and began to teach others about Jesus. Alma organized a church, and many people were baptized . . . all because God gave me the COURAGE to stand up for what is right. (Mosiah 17:4; Mosiah 18:1–3, 16–17)

How can YOU show courage like Abinadi?

THEN

NOW

"I can do all things through Christ which strengtheneth me."

Sometimes, you are put in situations where you need COURAGE to stand up for what is right.
What will you do?

If you will ask Him, Heavenly Father will give you the power to do the right thing and not be afraid even when it is not easy.

Some people will listen to you . . . and want to follow your example. Heavenly Father is always watching and is proud of you when you choose the right.

You CAN make a difference when you have the COURAGE to stand up for what is right.

93

FHE Lesson Helps for Abinadi Shows Courage

Songs and Hymns

Children's Songbook:
"Book of Mormon Stories," pp. 118–19 (vs. 4)
"Dare to Do Right," p. 158
"Stand for the Right," p. 159
"Choose the Right Way," p. 160

LDS Hymns:
"Choose the Right," no. 239
"True to the Faith," no. 254
"Who's on the Lord's Side?" no. 260

Scriptures on Having the Courage to Choose the Right

Joshua 24:15; Alma 30:8; Moses 6:33
Matthew 5:14–16; 3 Nephi 12:14–16
Romans 1:16
D&C 6:33
D&C 30:11

Note: You can put the scriptural references on sticky notes and attach them in the pages of this book where it describes Abinadi's courage. The children can find the sticky notes, look up the scripture (individually or as a family), and then discuss how the example applies to them.

Other Scripture Stories on This Topic

Shadrach, Meshach, and Abed-nego and the Fiery Furnace (Daniel 3)

Daniel in the Lion's Den (Daniel 6)

Quotes from General Authorities

"Will it take courage to stand tall? Of course it will. Can you muster the courage? Of course you can. Seek strength from your Heavenly Father."
    Bishop H. David Burton
    "Standing Tall," *Ensign*, November 2001, pp. 65–66.

"What a powerful example Abinadi should be to all of us! He courageously obeyed the Lord's commandments—even though it cost him his life!"
    Elder Robert D. Hales
    "'If Thou Wilt Enter into Life, Keep the Commandments,'" *Ensign*, May 1996, p. 35.

Stories and Messages from *The Friend* Magazine

"Courage Counts" (President Thomas S. Monson, *The Friend*, November 2005, pp. 2–3)

"Being Brave" (*The Friend*, January 2006, pp. 38–40)

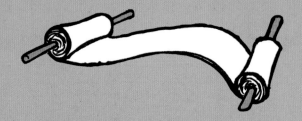

Activities

Write a Letter
Have each child write a letter to Abinadi, telling him how he or she has followed (or will follow) Abinadi's example by showing courage. The next family home evening, deliver letters to the children that "Abinadi" (aka—Mom or Dad) has written back to each child, commending them for their behavior.

You Draw the Story
Read the "How you can be like Abinadi" pages together. Then, have each child draw his or her own page of specific ways he or she can follow (or has recently followed) Abinadi's example by showing courage. Tuck the drawings into the book or put them on the refrigerator as reminders to try to be like Abinadi.

What Would You Do?
Review the two "How you can be like Abinadi" scenarios given (i.e. standing up for the girl getting picked on and not watching the R-rated movie). Ask each child to think of ways that he or she could stand up for the right in those two situations. Then, come up with additional, similar situations that the members of your family might encounter. Some examples might be—
 • Getting invited to a birthday party on Sunday
 • Other kids at school making fun of Mormons
 • Noticing somebody at school cheating on an assignment or test
 • Finding a lost wallet with money in it
Have the children act out the scenes, showing how they would respond.

As for Alma . . .
Everyone can think of a time they have felt like Alma—where they have seen and been impressed with someone else who stood up for the right in a tough situation. Mom and Dad can share their experiences with this and then invite the children to do the same (even better if their courageous examples happen to be other family members). Make sure you point out that even though only one of King Noah's priests listened to Abinadi, the effect that Abinadi's courage had on future generations was huge! (i.e. Alma—Alma the Younger—Helaman—Helaman—Nephi—Nephi, who was the prophet when Jesus visited the Americas).

A Fun Family Activity
Have family members sit on the floor, back-to-back, and try to stand up, using only the pressure from the other person's back (no arms). After successfully doing it in pairs, try it in groups of three . . . four . . . five . . . etc. Afterward, point out that it helps to have the support of other people to help you to "stand up" in a difficult situation, especially the support of your Heavenly Father . . . just as Abinadi had.

ALMA THE YOUNGER
Apologizes

Scripture Power!

Behold, he who has repented of his sins, the same is forgiven, and I, the Lord, remember them no more.

By this ye may know if a man repenteth of his sins—behold, he will confess them and forsake them.

—D&C 58:42-43

Hello, friend! My name is Alma. I was named after my father, and I am often called Alma, the younger.

I want to tell you about an experience I had that taught me how to APOLOGIZE. It required me to have a change of heart.

Before I had a change of heart, I was doing wicked things against what my parents had taught me. My actions were keeping others from feeling the Spirit and causing problems in the Church. The four sons of King Mosiah were following my bad example. (Mosiah 27:8–9)

My problem was—I had a **HARD** heart. When someone has a **HARD** heart, they don't want to be good. They don't want to obey or be reverent. The sons of Mosiah and I went from town to town getting into trouble. (Mosiah 27:10)

One day, an angel suddenly appeared right in front of us! We were so afraid. "Alma," he said with a loud voice, "you are disrupting the Lord's church and leading others to follow after your bad example!" (Mosiah 27:11–13)

"Your father has prayed with much faith for you to have a change of heart," the angel continued. "I am here to answer his prayers. So, Alma . . . GO THY WAY AND DISRUPT THE CHURCH NO MORE!" (Mosiah 27:14–16)

With that, the angel left. I was so astonished, I fell back to the ground. I couldn't speak or move my body. It was like I was asleep. (Mosiah 27:17–19)

The sons of Mosiah carried me to my father and told him what had happened. My father knew that his prayers had been answered and that the power of God was helping me to have a change of heart. (Mosiah 27:19–20)

For two whole days, I couldn't move or speak. Everyone fasted and prayed for me to get better. Finally, I woke up with . . . (Mosiah 27:21–23)

. . . a changed heart! My heart was no longer **HARD** . . . it was *Soft.* I had felt Jesus' love for me while I was asleep. That feeling made me want to be good and change my actions. Now, I needed to go back and APOLOGIZE to those I had harmed. (Mosiah 27:24–26, 27–31)

First, I told people I was sorry for how I had been acting. I really meant it, too! (Mosiah 27:35)

Next, I repaired anything that I had broken. If people's feelings had been hurt because of me, I tried to make things right again. I did this through my actions, not just my words. (Mosiah 27:35)

Finally, the sons of Mosiah and I went around helping people instead of causing trouble. We taught people about Jesus and tried to follow His example. Ever since I felt a change of heart and APOLOGIZED, I have been so much happier. (Mosiah 27:35–37)

How can YOU be like Alma the Younger?

THEN

NOW

"If a man repenteth of his sins—behold, he will confess them and forsake them."

Sometimes we have **HARD** hearts that cause us to be mean to others or make wrong choices. You need a *Soft* heart before you can really feel sorry for something you have done wrong. Remembering Jesus' love will help you have a *Soft* heart.

110

When your heart is soft you will want to APOLOGIZE to whomever you have hurt.

Then, try to make things right that you did wrong, even if it means sacrificing something of your own.

After you've APOLOGIZED, show more love toward that person. When you have a **Soft** heart, you will want to follow Jesus' example, and you will be happier.

FHE Lesson Helps for Alma the Younger Apologizes

Songs and Hymns

Children's Songbook:
  "Book of Mormon Stories," p. 118–119 (vs. 3)
  "I Feel My Savior's Love," p. 74
  "I'm Trying to Be like Jesus," p. 78
  "Choose the Right Way," p. 160

LDS Hymns:
  "Our Savior's Love," no. 113
  "Come unto Jesus," no. 117
  "Jesus, the Very Thought of Thee," no. 141

Scriptures on Apologizing and Having a Change of Heart

  1 Nephi 2:16
  Mosiah 3:19
  Mosiah 5:2, 7
  Mosiah 27:24–25
  Alma 5:12, 14

Note: You can put the scriptural references on sticky notes and attach them to the pages of this book where it describes Alma the Younger's change of heart. The children can find the sticky notes, look up the scripture (individually or as a family), and then discuss how the example applies to them.

Other Scripture Stories on This Topic

Paul's conversion (Acts 9)

Aaron helps convert King Lamoni's Father (Alma 22:1–26)

Quotes from General Authorities

"If we . . . sincerely repent, we will receive a spiritual change of heart which only comes from our Savior. Our hearts will become new again."
    Elder Robert D. Hales
    "Healing Soul and Body," *Ensign,* November 1998, p. 14.

"As individuals, we should 'follow after the things which make for peace' (Romans 14:19). We should be personal peacemakers."
    Elder Russell M. Nelson
    "Blessed Are the Peacemakers," *Ensign,* November 2002, p. 41.

Stories and Messages from *The Friend* Magazine

"I Can Repent and Be Happy" (*The Friend,* April 2006, p. 14—activity included)

"Heather Mends a Mistake" (*The Friend,* March 1988, p. 8)

"A New Heart" (*The Friend,* January 2006, p. 12)

Activities

WRITE A LETTER
Have each child write a letter to Alma telling him how he or she has followed (or will) follow his example by APOLOGIZING. Next family home evening, deliver letters to the children that "Alma" (aka—Mom or Dad) has written back to each child, commending them for their behavior.

YOU DRAW THE STORY
Read the "How can YOU be like Alma" pages together. Then, have each child draw his or her own page of specific ways he or she can follow (or has recently followed) Alma's example by APOLOGIZING. Tuck the drawings into the book or put them on the refrigerator as reminders to try to be like Alma.

PRACTICE MAKES PERFECT
Have family members write on slips of paper various situations where they would need to apologize. Draw slips out of a bowl and have children role-play how they would fully apologize in that situation. Use the Alma Application pages and the following formula to help.
> S— Say you're sorry (p. 111)
> O— Offer kindness (p. 113)
> R— Right the wrong (p. 112)
> R— Really mean it
> Y— You will feel happy!

You can make a "SORRY" poster and have the family repeat it several times to help with memorization. Offer a reward for memorizing it.

HARD HEART, ***SOFT*** HEART
Cut out a whole bunch of paper hearts. On the back of each heart, write either an example of a **HARD** heart (teasing siblings, arguing with parents, disobeying, etc.), or a ***Soft*** heart (apologizing, showing kindness, helping, etc.). Hide all the hearts throughout the room or house and have the children go find them. Each child shares (or acts out) his or her example, and the rest of the family identifies whether they are showing a hard or soft heart. Then . . .
—**HARD** hearts get crumpled up and thrown in the garbage (where they belong).
—***Soft*** hearts get stuck on each other (place a tape roll on the back). For extra fun, blindfold one of the children and play "pin the soft heart on your brother/sister" or "pin the soft heart on Alma." (Copy the picture on p. 168.)

HOW IS MY HEART TODAY?
Make a copy of the Alma picture (on p. 168) for each member of the family. Have them color their own and post them on the refrigerator or in their rooms. Each time they demonstrate a soft heart, add a "heart" (sticker or just draw one on) to their picture. At the end of a given period of time, have a ***Soft*** heart party (example: Eating heart shaped cookies while sitting on pillows) for those who earned a certain number of hearts.

AMULEK and ALMA
Cooperate

Scripture Power!

And the Lord called his people ZION, because they were of one heart and one mind, and dwelt in righteousness; and there was no poor among them.
—Moses 7:18

Hi there, I'm Amulek. Do you know what it means to COOPERATE? I learned all about cooperation while serving a mission with Alma. Let me tell you about it.

One day I was traveling to visit a relative when an angel suddenly appeared! "Amulek," he said, "return to your house, for you are going to feed a prophet of God. He is hungry and needs your help." I did what the angel told me to do. (Alma 10:7–8)

On my way home, I met the prophet, just like the angel said I would. His name was Alma and he had not had anything to eat for many days. I took him to my house and invited him to have dinner with us. He was very grateful. (Alma 8:19–20)

Alma ate dinner with my family and thanked us for being so kind to him. He said that he was commanded to help the people in my city repent of their wickedness. "And God wants *you*, Amulek, to preach with me and be my companion," Alma told me. I accepted the call. (Alma 8:21–29)

Alma and I went into the city and began talking to the people. We told them of the coming of Jesus Christ and that they needed to repent and turn to Jesus. The people were very prideful and did not want to hear this. (Alma 8:32; 9:1–8, 31–34)

Since we were companions, we took turns preaching to the people. Alma and I worked together to share God's message. (Alma 9:1–6, 34; 10:12; 12:1)

But even then they would not listen to us. Instead they were angry and threw Alma and me into pris-on. (Alma 14:2–4, 17)

We were in prison for many days. The wicked judges and priests mocked us. They hit us on our cheeks and gave us very little food and water. Alma and I supported each other during this very difficult time. (Alma 14:18–24)

After many days of this, the Lord filled us with his power. We stood up and Alma cried out, "O Lord, give us strength, according to our faith in Christ, to break these chains!" We snapped our chains and the whole prison began to shake! The judges and priests tried to escape, but the prison walls fell on top of them. (Alma 14:25–27)

Alma and I were the only ones to walk out of the collapsed prison. The Lord had kept us safe.

(Alma 14:28–29)

After that, Alma returned the kindness I had shown to him. He took me to *his* house and fed *me*. We had suffered so much together. It was nice to have a friend who cared. (Alma 15:16, 18)

Alma and I spent several years together as missionary companions. It was our job to go all over the land teaching the gospel of Jesus Christ. We were able to help many people because we knew how to COOPERATE with each other and work together. (Alma 16:13–15)

How can YOU be like Amulek and Alma?

THEN

NOW

ELDER AMULEK

"And the Lord called his people ZION, because they were of one heart and one mind"

Show kindness to everyone, even to people you don't know well. They will usually be kind to you in return.

Learn how to take turns with people . . . and be happy when it's their turn also.

Help other people even when things are stressful. Those are the times when we especially need to COOPERATE and not argue.

Any job can be fun when you work together and COOPERATE. And it sure makes the job easier!

FHE Lesson Helps for Amulek and Alma Cooperate

Songs and Hymns

Children's Songbook:
"Book of Mormon Stories," 118–19 (additional verse by David Bowman)

> *Amulek and Alma were great mission companions.*
> *Preaching side by side, they worked until the job was done.*
> *Cooperation was the key to their great success.*
> *They showed us that team work works the BEST!*

"A Happy Helper," 197
"I'll Walk with You," 140–41
"Kindness Begins with Me," 145

LDS Hymns:
"Let Us Oft Speak Kind Words," no. 232
"As Sisters in Zion," no. 309
"Love at Home," no. 294

Scriptures on Cooperating

Proverbs 18:24
1 Peter 3:8
Mosiah 2:17
3 Nephi 11:29
Moses 7:18

Other Scripture Stories on This Topic

David's and Jonathan's friendship (1 Samuel 18:1–4; 19:1–5; 20:4, 17)

The people of Nephi live in a spirit of cooperation (2 Nephi 5:9–18, 26–27)

Quotes from General Authorities

"Kindness is a passport that opens doors and fashions friends. It softens hearts and molds relationships that can last lifetimes."
> Elder Joseph B. Wirthlin
> "The Virtue of Kindness," *Ensign,* May 2005, 26

"Be that kind of friend and that kind of person who lifts and strengthens others."
> Elder Robert D. Hales
> "Gifts of the Spirit," *Ensign,* February 2002, 12

Stories and Messages from *The Friend* Magazine

"Getting Pushy on the Pond," Jean Leedale Hobson, January 2008, 46–47

"Who Is My Neighbor?" Ruth Kathryn Day, August 2007, 42–43

Activities

Let's Cooperate

Adjust these fun, simple cooperation activities for the size of your family. When you are finished doing them, discuss how working together to succeed at the games is much like the need for working together to succeed as a family.

Human Pyramid: You know how to do this one. Be careful who goes on which layer of the pyramid!

Three-or-More-Legged Race: A three-legged race is fun, but how much more fun (and more cooperation is needed) to succeed in a four-, five-, six-, or more-legged race!

Wheelbarrow Race: You know how to do this one, too. Be careful that the person pushing the wheelbarrow-person doesn't push too hard or too fast.

Feed Your Neighbor: Seated in a circle, eat dinner or dessert with each person's plate placed halfway between him or her and the person to their left. For the entire meal, each person has to feed the person to his left. No one is allowed to feed himself!

String Carry: Using only a piece of string, one person tries picking up an object (a block, book, etc.) by balancing the object on top of the stretched-out string. When he fails, try picking up the object the same way using two people and two pieces of string. Then try it with three, four, or five people—as many family members as you have (each adding another string). Each added person and string should make the task easier, giving more support underneath the object. Try carrying the object across the room.

Got Your Back: Sitting or standing in a circle, everyone gives the person in front of them a shoulder rub or back scratch. Aaahh, that feels good!

Back Stand: Have family members sit on the floor in pairs, back to back, and try to stand up using no arms but only the pressure from the other person's back. After successfully doing it in pairs, try it in groups of three, four, five, etc.

Puzzling Family

On a single sheet of paper, each family member draws a quick picture of himself or herself. Once the family portrait masterpiece is completed, Mom or Dad cuts the picture into pieces, writes one of the Scriptures on Cooperating* on the back of each piece, and gives one piece to each person. Family members look up their scriptures, taking turns reading them out loud and explaining what they mean to them. Then, one by one, they put their pieces back down, eventually completing the puzzle and putting the family back together! List specific ways your family could cooperate better. After family home evening, tape the picture pieces together and hang the portrait on the fridge as a reminder that "we don't want to be a separate-pieces family, but a joined-together family!"

* Other good scriptures are Colossians 3:19, 21 (for Dad's piece of the puzzle), Mosiah 4:14–15 (for Mom's piece), and Colossians 3:20 (for one of the children).

AMMON
Loves to Serve

Scripture Power!

And behold, I tell you these things that ye may learn wisdom; that ye may learn that when ye are in the service of your fellow beings ye are only in the service of your God.
—Mosiah 2:17

Hi, there, friend! My name is Ammon.

I am a Nephite. I want to tell you about my mission. That is where I learned the importance of SERVICE.

One day, my three brothers and I left our home to go be missionaries to a people called the Lamanites. The Lamanites did not like the Nephites. The Lamanites also did not know about Jesus. I wanted to teach them about Jesus so they could be happy. My brothers and I decided to split up. "Good-bye, brothers!" I waved. (Alma 17:12–19)

As I was walking across the Lamanite lands, some men grabbed me and took me to the king of the Lamanites. The king's name was Lamoni. "We do not like Nephites," said the king. "Why are you here?" (Alma 17:20–22)

"I want to be your servant," I told him. King Lamoni was very surprised that I only wanted to serve him. (Alma 17:23–25)

I was sent to help watch over the king's sheep. It was hard work, but it felt good being a helper. I did the best job I could. (Alma 17:25–26)

One day, as we were taking the sheep to get a drink, some bad men came and scared away all the sheep! (Alma 17:27)

The other servants were very worried! They knew the king would be angry with them because they had lost his sheep. "Don't worry, we'll find them," I said. We went looking, found all of the lost sheep, and rounded them up. (Alma 17:28–32)

But the bad men came BACK! I wasn't going to let them scare away the sheep again. I bravely went out to stop the bad men. I knew the Lord was with me. I was able to protect the sheep with my sword, and the bad men ran away. (Alma 17:33–39)

When the other servants hurried to tell the king what had happened, King Lamoni was amazed! He knew that the Lord was with me. "Where is Ammon now?" he asked. (Alma 18:1–8)

"He is feeding your horses," they answered. I had remembered that feeding the horses was another job that the king had asked me to do. I wanted to serve King Lamoni without being asked twice. (Alma 18:9)

King Lamoni was very pleased with me! "Ammon is my best servant!" he shouted. "He remembers to do all the things I ask him to do." (Alma 18:10)

Because of the faithful way I had served him, the king wanted to learn more about God. I taught him the gospel of Jesus Christ, and he and his family were baptized. Many of the other Lamanites also began to believe in Jesus. (Alma 18:39–40; 19:35–36)

How can YOU love serving like Ammon?

THEN

NOW

"When ye are in the service of your fellow beings ye are only in the service of your God."

Do chores around the house. Put your happy face on when you do them!

Help out with jobs in the yard. Do it without being asked twice!

Do nice things for other people, especially your brothers and sisters. Everyone will feel good!

Cheer up others who are sad. Invite them to play with you. Be friends with everyone!

FHE Lesson Helps for Ammon Loves to Serve

Songs and Hymns

Children's Songbook:
   "Book of Mormon Stories," pp. 118–19 (vs. 5)
   (change the word *live* to *serve*)
   "A Special Gift Is Kindness," p. 145
   "Kindness Begins with Me," p. 145
   "A Happy Helper," p. 197

LDS Hymns:
   "Love One Another," no. 308
   "Have I Done Any Good?" no. 223
   "Because I Have Been Given Much," no. 219

Scriptures on Serving Others

   Mosiah 2:17
   Matthew 25:40
   John 13:34–35
   James 1:27
   Deuteronomy 22:4

Note: You can put the scriptural references on sticky notes and attach them in the pages of this book where it describes Ammon's service. The children can find the sticky notes, look up the scripture (individually or as a family), and then discuss how the example applies to them.

Other Scriptural Stories on This Topic

The Good Samaritan (Luke 10:30–37)
Jesus Washing the Disciples' Feet (John 13:4–5, 12–17)

Quotes from the Prophets and Apostles

"Happiness comes through serving our Heavenly Father and serving our fellowmen."
   President Thomas S. Monson
      "Happiness through Service," *Ensign,* May 1988, p. 83.

"The greatest fulfillment in life comes by rendering service to others."
   President James E. Faust
      "What's in It for Me?" *Ensign,* November 2002, p. 22.

Stories and Messages from The Friend Magazine

"The Do-Gooders Club" (*The Friend,* March 2005, p. 4)

"Zucchini Bandit" (*The Friend,* July 2004, p. 44)

Activities

Write a Letter
Have each child write a letter to Ammon, telling him how he or she has followed (or will follow) Ammon's example by serving others. The next family home evening, deliver letters to the children that "Ammon" (aka—Mom or Dad) has written back to each child, commending them for their behavior.

You Draw the Story
Read the "How you can be like Ammon" pages together. Then, have each child draw his or her *own* page of specific ways he or she can follow (or has recently followed) Ammon's example by serving others. Tuck the drawings into the book or put them on the refrigerator as reminders to try to be like Ammon.

"Sheep"-ret Service (Secret Service)
Everyone draws several little individual sheep (or make several photocopies of this one, found on page 169). Cut them out and give each family member a stack of sheep. Next, everyone randomly picks a name out of a hat of another family member to be the one they will give "sheep"-ret service to that week. Then, during the week, each time someone does a secret act of service, (examples: make their bed, pick up their toys, give them a treat, etc.) that person leaves a little sheep cut-out behind to let them know that *they* have just been *"Sheep"-ret Serviced!* For EXTRA fun— Keep track of *who* is receiving *what* "sheep"-ret services on a chart . . . so everyone can monitor it. See who can *receive* the most service. At a later Family Home Evening, everyone reveals the name they have drawn.

The Love Seat
Put a chair (preferably a soft, cozy one) in the front of the room. This is now the "Love Seat." One by one, each member of the family takes a turn sitting on the Love Seat while the rest of the family cheers for him or her. While the honored person is seated there, every other family member thinks of *three* specific things they like about that person. Then, everyone shares *one* compliment at a time. Rules: you must look the honored person in the eye (no breaking eye contact allowed), call the person by name, share your compliment (and it must be nice!), and conclude by saying: "And *that* is one of the MANY reasons I love you!" The more you get into it, the more fun it will be . . . even for teenagers, believe it or not.

Blitz Mom!
Quick! For a specified duration of time—see how many things the family can do for Mom. Tidy up the house, do some dishes, clean rooms, vacuum, dust, massage Mom's feet . . . *whatever* she wants, as fast as you can, during the allotted time. While she is being "blitzed," the only thing Mom is allowed to do is recline in a comfortable chair and breathe sighs of contentment.

ABISH
Acts on Inspiration

Hello, there. I'm Abish. I want to tell you about a time I helped others believe in God because I acted on inspiration.

Scripture Power!

Yea, behold, I will tell you in your mind and in your heart, by the Holy Ghost, which shall come upon you and which shall dwell in your heart.

Now, behold, this is the spirit of revelation; behold, this is the spirit by which Moses brought the children of Israel through the Red Sea on dry ground.
—D&C 8:2-3

I am a servant to the Lamanite king and queen. A Nephite missionary named Ammon had been teaching King Lamoni about the Lord and His gospel. I already had a testimony of the gospel and was excited to see my king learning about it too. (Alma 18:36, 39)

One day, I went into King Lamoni's chambers and found him, the queen, Ammon, and the other servants all lying on the ground as if they were dead. Woa! But I knew they weren't actually dead. Instead, they had fallen down because the power of God was changing their hearts. ***This gave me an idea...*** (Alma 19:16-17)

I ran from house to house, telling everyone what had just happened. I wanted them to come and see what the power of God had just done. I thought this might help them believe in God too. (Alma 19:17)

However, when the people saw the scene, some were scared. Others were confused. Still, others were angry. Instead of believing it was God's power they saw, they began to argue with each other about what this meant. (Alma 19:18-19, 25-27)

"Oh, no!" I thought. "I had better do something!" Which gave me an idea... I reached down and took the queen's hand, hoping that she would wake up if I touched her. And guess what? She did wake up! Phew. (Alma 19:28-29)

The queen stood up and began telling the people that the Lord had just changed her heart. Then King Lamoni, Ammon, and the servants all stood up and bore their testimonies. The people who listened felt the Spirit and began to believe in God. It was amazing! I was so glad that I had acted on inspiration. (Alma 19:29-36)

162

How can YOU act on inspiration like Abish?

THEN

NOW

"I will tell you in your mind and in your heart, by the Holy Ghost"

Do YOU ever get ideas of good things you can do or ways you can help someone? Those ideas come from the Holy Ghost. It's called receiving promptings. Always pay attention to those promptings. Don't ignore them!

164

Then ACT on those ideas! Do those good deeds, even if they seem unusual or if no one else is doing it. Those small, simple promptings can help great things to happen.

165

Word Search

S	O	C	J	I	H	A	M	O	B	I	E	T	S	A
R	T	A	P	O	W	D	A	N	D	C	L	P	E	P
U	M	I	G	O	F	B	Z	P	N	Q	O	R	L	Y
A	W	F	C	R	H	I	I	E	U	M	C	B	T	U
P	P	U	R	O	L	B	R	S	E	P	D	I	S	K
N	E	L	T	I	N	E	M	E	H	R	E	B	O	N
O	A	A	V	P	F	O	N	Z	S	O	O	L	P	B
F	R	I	E	N	D	C	R	D	I	P	P	G	A	L
R	L	D	O	T	M	Y	E	E	C	H	M	O	S	E
I	A	C	B	D	O	L	O	O	V	E	O	T	Z	S
E	D	B	H	I	B	X	A	A	P	T	T	Y	I	S
N	R	O	M	I	R	A	U	L	E	B	P	A	D	I
N	E	F	B	O	O	K	O	F	M	O	R	M	O	N
O	N	O	I	T	A	L	E	V	E	R	L	J	O	G
T	D	A	I	B	S	H	O	N	O	P	E	C	A	S

Different sources where we can find the word of God:

PROPHET

APOSTLES

(General) CONFERENCE

BIBLE

BOOK OF MORMON

D AND C

PEARL (of Great Price)

FRIEND (magazine)

REVELATION

BISHOP

How is YOUR heart today?

169

About the Author/Illustrator

Following his service as a full-time missionary in the Philippines, David Bowman graduated with a degree in illustration from Brigham Young University. He has since served as a release-time seminary instructor as well as a counselor and speaker at numerous EFY conferences. His special love is making the scriptures come to life for young people.

David is the author/illustrator of the bestselling *Who's Your Hero? Book of Mormon Stories Applied to Children* series. His other books include *The Great Plan of Happiness; Dude, Don't Be a Lemuel: A Teenage Guide to Avoiding Lemuelitis;* and *What Would the Founding Fathers Think? A YOUNG Americans Guide to Understanding What Makes Our Nation Great and How We've Strayed.*

He and his wife, Natalie, and their five children live in Arizona.

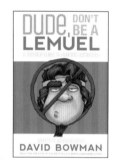

For more Who's Your Hero? fun stuff, products, bonus material, etc. go to

www.whosyourherobooks.com

David Bowman is also the artist of the "Expressions of Christ" series. You can see his fine-art depictions of the Savior, as well as his other books, at

www.davidbowmanart.com